GALE
CENGAGE Learning

Nonfiction Classics for Students, Volume 1

Staff

Editor: Elizabeth Thomason.

Contributing Editors: Reginald Carlton, Anne Marie Hacht, Michael L. LaBlanc, Ira Mark Milne, Jennifer Smith.

Managing Editor, Literature Content: Dwayne D. Hayes.

Managing Editor, Literature Product: David Galens.

Publisher, Literature Product: Mark Scott.

Content Capture: Joyce Nakamura, *Managing Editor*. Sara Constantakis, *Editor*.

Research: Victoria B. Cariappa, *Research Manager*. Cheryl Warnock, *Research Specialist*. Tamara Nott, Tracie A. Richardson, *Research Associates*. Nicodemus Ford, Sarah Genik, Timothy Lehnerer, Ron Morelli, *Research Assistants*.

Copyright Notice

agency, institution, publication, service, or individual does not imply endorsement of the editors or publisher. Errors brought to the attention of the publisher and verified to the satisfaction of the publisher will be corrected in future editions.

This publication is a creative work fully protected by all applicable copyright laws, as well as by misappropriation, trade secret, unfair competition, and other applicable laws. The authors and editors of this work have added value to the underlying factual material herein through one or more of the following: unique and original selection, coordination, expression, arrangement, and classification of the information. All rights to this publication will be vigorously defended.

Pilgrim at Tinker Creek

Annie Dillard 1974

Introduction

Pilgrim at Tinker Creek, published in 1974, is a nonfiction work that defies categorization. The winner of the Pulitzer Prize for general nonfiction, it is often read as an example of American nature writing or as a meditation. Annie Dillard, the author, resists these labels, preferring to think of the book as a theological treatise. The book is frequently described as a collection of essays, but Dillard insists that the work is an integrated whole. Perhaps it is because the book succeeds on so many levels that it has been so widely read and admired.

The book is a series of internal monologues and reflections spoken by an unnamed narrator. Over the course of a year, she walks alone through the land surrounding Tinker Creek, located in the Blue Ridge Mountains near Roanoke, Virginia. As she observes the changing of the seasons and the corresponding behaviors of the plants and animals around her, she reflects on the nature of the world and of the God who set it in motion. The narrator is determined to present the natural world as it truly is, not sentimentally or selectively. Therefore, she is as likely to reflect on a frog being sucked dry by an insect as on the slant of light that strikes a certain springtime tree. Whether the images are cruel or lovely, the language is beautiful and poetic, and insistently celebratory.

Author Biography

Meta Ann Doak was born into an upper-middle-class family on April 30, 1945, in Pittsburgh, Pennsylvania. She and her two younger sisters were raised under the influences of their free-thinking parents, their wealthy paternal grandparents who lived nearby, and an African-American domestic servant. "Annie" was encouraged from the beginning to think and act independently, to tell stories, and to read books. She took piano and dance lessons, socialized at the country club, and attended the Ellis School, a private school for girls where she studied Latin, French, and German. But she had a keen interest in the natural world even as a girl, and assembled collections of rocks, bugs, and other elements of nature, as well as a collection of favorite poems. Dillard has recounted her early years in an autobiography, *An American Childhood* (1987).

Dillard's high school years were turbulent. Like many teenagers, she took up smoking and driving fast, and wrote angry poetry about the hypocrisy and emotional impoverishment of the adults around her. For a time, she even stopped attending the Presbyterian Church she had belonged to since childhood, but she soon felt the loss and returned. Dillard's struggle to understand God and religion and her fascination with poetic language— even her smoking—surface throughout her writing, including *Pilgrim at Tinker Creek*.

After high school, Dillard attended Hollins College, a women's college near Roanoke, Virginia, and studied creative writing and religion. At the end of her sophomore year, she married one of her creative writing professors, Richard Dillard. Richard was a strong influence on her writing, encouraging her to develop her skills as a poet and a natural historian. During the marriage, Dillard finished her undergraduate degree in English literature and completed a master's. The topic of her master's thesis was Henry David Thoreau's *Walden; or, Life in the Woods* (1854). Later, she would use *Walden* as the model for *Pilgrim at Tinker Creek*.

For the next few years, Dillard painted, wrote poetry, read widely, volunteered at local community agencies, and kept extensive journals of her observations and thoughts. In 1973, she turned those journals into *Pilgrim at Tinker Creek*, working as many as fifteen hours a day to complete the manuscript. She described the process of writing the book in *The Writing Life* (1989). Individual chapters of *Pilgrim* were published as essays in influential magazines, and when the full book was published in 1974, it was an immediate success. The book won the 1975 Pulitzer Prize for general nonfiction. At the time, Annie Dillard was just thirty years old. She eventually divorced Dillard and, in 1980, married writer Gary Clevidence.

Over the past quarter century, Dillard has published eight more books, including a novel, two collections of poetry, and several nonfiction volumes. These books have been well received, but

Dillard is still known primarily as the author of *Pilgrim at Tinker Creek*. She married another professor and writer, Robert D. Richardson Jr. in 1988.

Chapter One: "Heaven and Earth in Jest"

The opening of *Pilgrim at Tinker Creek* is one of the most famous passages from the book. "I used to have a cat," the book begins. The narrator reports that she was in the habit of sleeping naked in front of an open window, and the cat would use that window to return to the house at night after hunting. In the morning, the narrator would awaken to find her body "covered with paw prints in blood; I looked as though I'd been painted with roses."

This opening passage introduces several important ideas and approaches that will operate through the entire book. Dillard insistently presents the natural world as both beautiful and cruel, like the image of roses painted in blood. She demonstrates throughout the book that to discover nature, one must actively put oneself in its way. The narrator sleeps naked, with the windows open, to put no barriers between herself and the natural world. But the natural world is a manifestation of God, and it is God she is really seeking to understand through the book. Dillard introduces the theme of religion as the narrator washes the bloodstains off her body, wondering whether they are "the keys to the kingdom or the mark of Cain." Finally, the anecdote structure itself is typical;

throughout the book, Dillard weaves together passages of reflection, description, and narration.

The book's structure is loosely chronological, moving from January to December. "Heaven and Earth in Jest" is set in January, and several passages in present tense read like a naturalist's journal. But Dillard freely uses memories from other seasons and other years. "I am no scientist. I explore the neighborhood," the narrator says, explaining both her method and her purpose.

Chapter Two: "Seeing"

The ten sections of chapter two all explore the question of what it means to really see. The narrator explains how she has trained herself to see insects in flight, hidden birds in trees, and other common occurrences in nature that most people miss because the events are too small or happen too quickly. She spends hours on a log watching for muskrats and brings home pond water to study under a microscope. In a long passage, she tells about patients who benefitted from the first cataract operations, and their difficulties in trying to see with their eyes after a lifetime of blindness. As the narrator contemplates different ways of seeing, she realizes, "I cannot cause light; the most I can do is try to put myself in the path of its beam."

Chapter Three: "Winter"

"Winter" begins on the first of February with

the movements of large flocks of starlings that live in the area. Down by the creek, the narrator watches a coot and thinks about the frogs and turtles asleep under the mud. Her forays outside are shorter, and she spends evenings in front of the fireplace reading books about travel and about nature. Her only companions are a goldfish named Ellery Channing (after a friend of Henry David Thoreau) and the spiders that are allowed "the run of the house."

Chapter Four: "The Fixed"

In this chapter, the narrator discusses insects and stars. She has learned to recognize praying mantis egg cases in the wild, and she has brought one home and tied it to a branch near her window so she can observe the hatching. In the cold of February, she thinks about June and the steadiness of insects and the seeming fixedness of the stars.

Chapter Five: "Untying the Knot"

This short chapter takes its title from a snake skin the narrator finds in the woods. The skin appears to be tied in a knot, continuous, as the seasons are "continuous loops." The narrator contemplates the changing of the seasons and hopes to be alert and notice the exact moment when winter becomes spring.

Chapter Six: "The Present"

It is March. Surprisingly, as the chapter opens,

the narrator is at a gas station on an interstate highway, talking with the station attendant. But it is not the conversation that is important; rather, the narrator focuses on a beagle puppy, whose fur she rubs as she sips her coffee. For a moment, she feels entirely alive: "This is it, I think, this is it, right now, the present, this empty gas station here, this western wind, this tang of coffee on the tongue, and I am patting the puppy, I am watching the mountain."

The narrator reflects on human consciousness and self-consciousness, which act against being in the present and against being in the presence of God. She affirms her intention to push away connections with cities, with people. The flowing creek is new every second, and it is in the creek that grace can be found.

Chapter Seven: "Spring"

Spring unfolds through April and May, and the narrator has missed spring's beginning. Plants are greening and flowering, and hibernating animals are reappearing. The narrator feels an urgency to examine every creature quickly before summer comes and they begin to decay and devour each other.

Chapter Eight: "Intricacy"

This chapter contains more meditation than anecdote. In June, the narrator ponders the smallest things—red blood cells in a goldfish's tail, blooming plankton, the horsehair worm, molecules, and atoms. In the intricacy of the universe, she finds confirmation of God's presence and plan: "Beauty itself is the fruit of the creator's exuberance that grew such a tangle."

Chapter Nine: "Flood"

Like many of Dillard's chapter titles, "The Flood" is meant to be taken both literally and figuratively. This chapter, which opens with the first day of summer, describes an actual flooding of Tinker Creek and its effects on the landscape, the animals, and the narrator's human neighbors. It is among the most consistently narrative chapters of the book. The rising water brings with it a flood of emotions and thoughts, leaving the narrator feeling "dizzy, drawn, mauled."

Chapter Ten: "Fecundity"

Fecundity means "fruitfulness," and this chapter explores plants and animals, including fish, poppies, field mice, and bamboo, that grow quickly or produce large numbers of offspring. Of course, these creatures are so prolific because they must be: of a million fish eggs laid, only a few will survive to hatch. "What kind of a world is this, anyway," the narrator asks. "Are we dealing in life, or in death?"

Chapter Eleven: "Stalking"

As summer progresses, the narrator practices her skills at stalking animals, especially animals that do not wish to be seen, including fish, herons, and muskrats. As she watches fish, she thinks about fish as an ancient symbol for Christ and for the spirit. In a long passage, she describes how she has spent years learning to stalk muskrats. But stalking animals is not the end in itself: "You have to stalk the spirit, too."

Chapter Twelve: "Nightwatch"

In late summer, the narrator watches grasshoppers and locusts. She takes a sleeping bag and a sandwich to spend a night outside. As she watches the sunset and listens to the night sounds, she thinks, "this is my city, my culture, and all the world I need."

Chapter Thirteen: "The Horns of the Altar"

At mid-September, the narrator ponders poisons, parasites, and pests. In the natural world, creatures eat one another or die of other causes. The chapter title refers to altars used for sacrifices in the Old Testament of the Judeo-Christian Bible. Animals to be sacrificed would be tied to "horns," or rising side pieces, so that they would be suspended above burning coals. The narrator is aware of herself as a potential sacrifice, as eventual food for maggots and parasites. "I am aging and eaten and have done my share of eating too."

Chapter Fourteen: "Northing"

As October and November pass, the narrator thinks about heading north, facing directly into the coming winter. Watching butterflies and geese migrating south, she wishes to go north, to find a place where the wind and the view will be unimpeded, where she can find an austere simplicity. She believes that stillness will open her up to the presence of God.

Chapter Fifteen: "The Waters of Separation"

At the winter solstice, the weather is unusually warm. The narrator wanders through the brown landscape following a bee and reflecting on the year that has passed. The chapter title refers to ceremonial water used in the Old Testament for purifying the unclean. For Dillard, Tinker Creek flows with "the waters of beauty and mystery" and also with the waters of separation. In contemplating the natural world, she approaches God but separates herself from other people and from the things of this world. She drinks of this water willingly and with thanks.

Key Figures

The Narrator

    Pilgrim at Tinker Creek is written in the first person; that is, the narrator continually refers to herself as "I." But the book is not an autobiography, and the author is not the narrator. In fact, an early draft of the manuscript was set in New England and was narrated by a young man. For Dillard, the identity of the speaker was not central to her explorations. The narrator of *Pilgrim at Tinker Creek*, then, may more properly be thought of as a persona than as Dillard herself.

    Few biographical details can be discerned about the narrator. She lives near Tinker Creek in the Blue Ridge Mountains of Virginia. She is well-educated and has read widely, and she spends most of her time alone, closely observing the natural world. She seems to have no daily responsibilities or occupations, but has the time and the patience to spend hours alone in one place watching the light changing or a duck eating. She once had a cat, but she does not mention any family, and she does not seek the company of other humans except for an occasional evening game of pinochle with unnamed friends. No other person plays a significant role in the book.

Themes

Faith and Spirituality

As the first word of the title suggests, *Pilgrim at Tinker Creek* is primarily a book about seeking God. A "pilgrim" may be merely a person who travels, but more commonly the word is used to describe someone who travels to a holy place. For the narrator, the creek itself is as sacred as a church; it is here that she encounters God's grace in its purest form: "So many things have been shown me on these banks, so much light has illumined me by reflection here where the water comes down, that I can hardly believe that this grace never flags." In using water as a symbol of God's presence and grace, Dillard is drawing on centuries of religious tradition.

Throughout the book, Dillard balances the seemingly opposing forces of heaven and Earth, of God as the creator of beauty and of horror. Much of the imagery in the book is of the beauty and complexity of nature, reflecting God's grace. In every sunset, every egg case, every snake skin, the narrator sees God's generosity. But at times, reading about a praying mantis that has devoured her mate or contemplating hoards of parasites, she rails against the cruelties of nature, asking, "What kind of a world is this, anyway?" She wonders whether the mystery of cruelty is not part of God's plan. "It could be," she muses, that God has spread "a fabric of spirit and sense so grand and subtle, so powerful in a new way, that we can only feel blindly of its hem." She seems to conclude that, ultimately, humans must accept the contradictions of this world —must embrace death and darkness as part of the cycle of life and light.

Dillard has carefully studied the Bible, as demonstrated by the many biblical quotations and allusions throughout the book. But essential to Dillard's vision is the belief that the natural world is also a vehicle for spiritual insight. Just as the narrator has had to train herself to stalk wild animals to be in their presence, so she must also stalk God, seeking Him out where He is and as He is.

Individual and Society

A recurring idea in *Pilgrim at Tinker Creek* is the narrator's belief that she must choose between embracing nature and embracing human society. In fact, she does not seem to have close ties with any living humans. She alludes occasionally to playing baseball or pinochle—games that cannot be played in solitude—but she never names her companions. She is aware of neighborhood boys, and she knows the names of the people who own the property along Tinker Creek and of those who are endangered by the flood. But there is no strong feeling, positive or negative, expressed in any of her human contacts. While a puppy or a sunrise can leave her breathless, people do not.

Media Adaptations

- *Pilgrim at Tinker Creek* was published as an unabridged audio book by the American Library Association in 1995. The reading is by Barbara Rosenblat.

- Another unabridged edition on audiocassette, read by Grace Conlin, was produced by Blackstone Audio Books in 1993. This version is no longer available on cassettes, but http://www.audible.com offers it for sale as a downloadable file.

Her isolation is both inevitable and intentional. On the one hand, she feels unlike other people. She does not know others who rhapsodize as she does over slugs and spiders, and at times she feels like "a freak." More importantly, she has willed herself to be alone, to live in the world of nature instead of the world of the city. She has experienced both, and remembers in "The Present" the "human companionship, major-league baseball, and a clatter of quickening stimulus like a rush from strong drugs that leaves you drained." But human connection is a distraction, making it difficult to live in the present. In the same chapter, she almost drifts away into a memory of dancing and music years before, and she forcefully wills herself to abandon the memory: "I stir. The heave of my shoulders returns me to the present … and I yank myself away, shove off, seeking live water."

Although the persona who explores Tinker Creek from January to December 1972 lives alone with only goldfish and spiders for company, Annie Dillard was married and living with her husband at the time she wrote the book. She spent a great deal of time volunteering in her community, meeting with a writing group, and socializing with friends. The solitude of the narrator is, therefore, an intentional creation of the writer. As the narrator explains in "Fecundity," "I must go down to the creek again. It is where I belong, although as I become closer to it, my fellows appear more and more freakish, and my home in the library more and more limited. Imperceptibly at first, and now consciously, I shy away from the arts, from the human emotional stew."

Topics for Further Study

- Find out more about the Roman Catholic monk Thomas Merton, who was also a poet and a political activist. What causes did he speak out about? How did he understand the ideal balance between a life of contemplation and a life of activism?

- Read some excerpts from Henry David Thoreau's *Walden; or, Life in the Woods,* especially one or two passages in which he gives detailed accounts of his observations of nature. In terms of the amount of precise detail, how do his accounts compare with Dillard's? How would you compare the conclusions Thoreau and Dillard draw from their observations?

- For a short time, Dillard considered submitting her manuscript to publishers under the name "A. Dillard" so the publishers would assume the author was a man. Do you think this would have fooled them? If you did not know the name of the author of *Pilgrim at Tinker Creek*, what clues in the text would suggest a female author? Consider language, imagery, and attitude.

- Using balls to represent the Earth and the Sun, demonstrate the meanings of the terms "winter solstice" and "summer solstice." Explain how the position of the Earth relative to the Sun at each solstice affects the weather where you live.

- Spend an hour or more alone, replicating one of Dillard's activities: Stalk a muskrat or other animal to see how close you can get; sit still outside at sunrise or sunset and watch the light change; or pat a puppy and try to think of nothing else except what you are doing. Write a brief essay in which you describe the experience.

Nature

Although it does not seem to be what Dillard intended, *Pilgrim at Tinker Creek* is perhaps most frequently read as a piece of nature writing. The book is filled with narratives, descriptions, and unusual facts about a catalog of plants and animals. Some of the most famous passages in the book come from the writer's own observations; for example the description of the tomcat with bloody paws, the frog being sucked dry by a giant water bug, or the young muskrat floating on its back. Dillard is just as vivid when her narrator is retelling an observation she has read somewhere else: J. Henri Fabre's caterpillars walking a never-ending circular trail around the mouth of a vase, or his female praying mantis mating with a male whose head she has already eaten. For many readers, these glimpses of the world outside are valuable in themselves, without symbolizing anything beyond the literal.

On a practical level, the reader of *Pilgrim at Tinker Creek* learns a great deal about the natural world, primarily about the flora and fauna in the area around Tinker Creek. Readers who care to learn may gather enough information to begin their own explorations—to identify a monarch butterfly pupa or a sycamore tree. They may also put together an impressive reading list of some of the books from which Dillard has taught herself. Dillard combines her own observations with those of other writers to produce a record of the changing natural world through the calendar year, from January to

December. In doing so, and in making it seem so beautiful and fascinating, she encourages the reader to do the same. Dillard has learned much of her natural history from reading books, and her own book similarly instructs her readers.

Science and Technology

As she pieces together an understanding of God and the natural world, the narrator also considers what science can and cannot tell her. Repeatedly, she looks through microscopes or telescopes, using technology to see things that the naked eye cannot reveal. Several of her stories, including the account of the caterpillars following each other around the rim of a vase, demonstrate knowledge gained through scientific experimentation. In her acceptance of animal behavior in all its seeming cruelty, the narrator exhibits a scientist's objectivity. But she is fully aware of the limits of science. In "Stalking," for example, she discusses the principle of indeterminacy, which governs the study of atomic particles. The more scientists learn, she says, the more they become aware that they can never truly know: "we know now for sure that there is no knowing.... The use of instruments and the very fact an observer seem to bollix [bungle]the observations; as a consequence, physicists are saying that they cannot study nature per se, but only their own investigation of nature."

Dillard comes back to the limits of science

several times throughout Pilgrim at Tinker Creek. Ultimately, the impossibility of knowing everything both frustrates and comforts the narrator. She would like to find things out, and she keeps returninging to books and to observation, but she will never know it all. On the other hand, the very fact of the world being beyond human comprehension is, for her, confirmation of the existence of God.

Style

Structure

The fifteen essays or chapters of *Pilgrim at Tinker Creek* are organized into two parallel structures. The more obvious structure follows the calendar year from January, in the chapters "Heaven and Earth in Jest" and "Seeing," through spring, summer, and autumn to December 21 in the last chapter, "The Waters of Separation." The book is meant to resemble a polished journal that the narrator kept of her observations through one year, but in fact, the material was pulled together from twenty volumes of journals that Dillard kept over several years. The calendar year structure, describing the changes in the seasons, is a convention of American nature writing that has been used by Henry David Thoreau, Edwin Way Teale, Henry Beston, Aldo Leopold, and others.

A less obvious structure has been pointed out by Dillard herself and supports her insistence that the book be read as a whole, not as a collection of essays. As quoted in Sandra Humble Johnson's *The Space Between: Literary Epiphany in the Work of Annie Dillard,* Dillard explains that the structure of the book follows the path of the medieval mystic toward God. The first seven chapters represent the *via positiva,* or "the journey to God through action & will & materials." In these chapters, Dillard focuses on the beauty and intricacy of nature. After a meditative eighth chapter, "Intricacy," the last seven chapters represent the *via negativa,* or "the spirit's revulsion at time and death." In this half of the book, beginning with the destruction of "Flood," Dillard's anecdotes are more negative, focusing more on parasites, poisons, and death.

Setting

Pilgrim at Tinker Creek is set, as the title suggests, "by a creek, Tinker Creek, in a valley in Virginia's Blue Ridge" in the year 1972. The creek is outside the small town of Hollins, home of Hollins College. Dillard completed her bachelor's and master's degrees at Hollins College and lived near Tinker Creek for nine years in the late 1960s and early 1970s. Although the book appears to be a factual representation of place and time, the real Tinker Creek is not so isolated and wild as readers may assume. Through careful selection of detail, Dillard makes the area seem quiet, undeveloped, and largely uninhabited. Compare the impression of wilderness Dillard creates for this book to the way she describes the same locations in a later essay, "Living Like Weasels": "This is, mind you, suburbia. It is a five-minute walk in three directions to rows of houses, though none is visible here. There's a 55 m.p.h. highway at one end of the pond, and a nesting pair of wood ducks at the other.... The far end is an alternating series of fields and woods, fields and woods, threaded everywhere with motorcycle tracks." For *Pilgrim,* she has narrowed her focus to specific moments and specific images, leaving out the details that work against her purpose. The setting of *Pilgrim at Tinker Creek* is, therefore, a slightly fictionalized version of a real place.

Similarly, the book appears to record the events of one calendar year, 1972. Obviously, the chapters also include information from the narrator's reading and from her past. The stories from her own past are clearly tagged with phrases like "several years ago" or "once." These narratives are written in the past tense. Narratives that are meant to be immediate ("I am sitting") or very recent ("yesterday") are presented as though they occurred in the order told and within one year. These observations actually occurred over a period of several years.

Although *Pilgrim at Tinker Creek* is classified as nonfiction, it has elements of fiction in its setting. It has the appearance of a journal or an autobiography, but it is not one. Rather, it is a series of reflections set into a journal form.

Figurative Language

One of the most admired qualities of *Pilgrim at Tinker Creek* is the beauty and power of its language. Dillard studied creative writing at Hollins College and has published two volumes of poetry. Her concern with figurative or "poetic" language is apparent on every page. Because nature is so evocative for Dillard, she uses grand language to describe it, particularly when she is awed. Describing her reaction to "the tree with the lights in it," she writes, "The vision comes and goes, mostly goes, but I live for it, for the moment when the mountains open and a new light roars in spate through the crack, and the mountains slam." In this line, she is speaking metaphorically, especially with the verbs "open," "roars" and "slam." The line is made more powerful by the repetition of "comes and goes, mostly goes" and "I live for it, for the moment," and the unusual word "spate" elevates the line further. This line and countless others like it strike many readers as more like poetry than like prose.

The 1960s and 1970s

The years during which Dillard lived in the Blue Ridge Mountains, keeping her journals and writing *Pilgrim at Tinker Creek*, were among the most turbulent in recent United States history. In the five years before she began writing in 1973, civil rights leader Martin Luther King, Jr., and presidential candidate Robert F. Kennedy were assassinated; the United States withdrew from Vietnam after a long and unsuccessful military action in which tens of thousands of Americans died; the presidency of Richard Nixon had started to unravel because of the scandal known as "Watergate"; the nation was feeling the first effects of an energy crisis; an Equal Rights Amendment to the U.S. Constitution, addressing gender equality issues, was passed by Congress but never ratified by the states.

It is striking, then—and for some critics at the time it was disturbing—that Dillard mentions none of these things in her book. Dillard's focus is both inward and outward, but her concerns are spiritual, not social or political. She is aware of what is going on in the world; she pores over the newspapers and spends time in the library. She reads and admires the monk Thomas Merton, who balanced a contemplative life with activism against nuclear weapons. But Dillard chooses in this work to direct her gaze away from social concerns, as she explains in "Intricacy": "I would like to see it all, to understand it, but I must start somewhere, so I try to deal with the giant water bug in Tinker Creek and the flight of three hundred redwings from an Osage orange, with the goldfish bowl and the snakeskin, and let those who dare worry about the birthrate and population explosion among solar systems."

Nature Writing

Although *Pilgrim at Tinker Creek* has proven difficult for readers to categorize, it is most often located in the genre of nature writing. Nature writing is not so strictly defined as the sonnet or the novel, but there are several criteria that critics agree upon. Generally, nature writing is nonfiction prose set in the wilderness or in a rural area. Its primary focus is on accurate but beautifully rendered descriptions of the natural phenomena that occur in one limited place, not on political or social commentary. The speaker or narrator of a piece of nature writing reports her own observations; she does not interfere with nature, but carefully and patiently records every detail. Most importantly, she is well-educated and checks her facts. It is not enough to write gushing prose about the beauty of a heron at sunset; the nature writer must have enough scientific knowledge to place the scene in its biological, climatological, and even cosmological context.

Early English writers, who lacked what we would consider today to be basic scientific knowledge of the world, must have found nature to be as unpredictable and frightening as it was beautiful and awe-inspiring. They did not know much about the natural world except how it affected them, and in accordance with Judeo-Christian thought of the time, they believed that humans were set apart from nature by God—apart from it and above it. Images of nature in literature tended to be used as a backdrop for more important human activity, or as a symbol of human emotions and spirit. In these works, nature exists to serve and to represent humans. Details about flowers or birds or mountains tend to be vague and impressive, rather than detailed and accurate. Writers and readers alike had little knowledge about the behavior of muskrats, and little interest in obtaining more. What was more important was what a muskrat could represent—mystery, or industry, or beauty, or danger.

Compare & Contrast

- **1970:** On April 22, the first Earth Day is observed, marking a strong interest in environmental issues across the United States.

  Today: Although a small group of environmental advocates tries to create a sensation, the thirtieth anniversary of Earth Day receives scant attention in the nation's newspapers.

- **1974:** Dillard considers submitting her manuscript of *Pilgrim at Tinker Creek* under the name "A. Dillard," because she does not believe that a book with theological themes written by a woman will sell many copies.

  Today: Although publications by men still out number those by women in the fields of religion and philosophy, women are accepted as making important contributions in these disciplines.

- **1975:** Environmental literature is popular with general readers and with critics. Annie Dillard wins the Pulitzer Prize for general nonfiction for *Pilgrim at Tinker Creek* and Gary Snyder wins the Pulitzer Prize for poetry for *Turtle Island,* a collection of nature poems.

  Today: Nature writers including Terry Tempest Williams, Rick Bass, and Ann Zwinger reach a small but dedicated readership.

In the nineteenth century, however, two important books changed the way writers and others looked at the natural world, and became the origins of what is today called nature writing or environmental literature. The first book, published in 1845, by Henry David Thoreau, was *Walden, or, Life in the Woods. Walden,* considered one of the classic works of American literature, is an account of two years Thoreau spent living in a small cabin on the shore of Walden Pond near Concord, Massachusetts. Thoreau combines passages of reflection on daily life, government, and society with passages of close examination of worms and beans and rain. Others had looked at nature objectively, and for its own sake, without attributing human characteristics to it, but Thoreau's work was so beautifully written and clearly argued that it reached a large audience and endured.

The second important book was Charles Darwin's 1859 *On the Origin of Species by Means of Natural Selection, or the Preservation of Favoured Races in the Struggle for Life.* Darwin's book proposed for the first time that humans, and all living creatures, have evolved over time from previous species. It is difficult for us today to understand how shocking this idea was for Darwin's first readers. Darwin was saying that humans are not above nature, but a part of it; he claimed that life has evolved in a continuing pattern, rather than being set down on earth for the pleasure and use of humans. With this new sense of nature and human-kind's role in it, there came a new interest in studying and classifying the natural world, in understanding it on its own terms.

The tradition of nature writing in the United States can be traced to the journals and essays of the earliest explorers in the New World. The most important works include Henry David Thoreau's *Walden; or, Life in the Woods* (1845); John Muir's *The Mountains of California* (1894); Mary Austin's *The Land of Little Rain* (1903); and Aldo Leopold's *A Sand County Almanac* (1949). The last third of the twentieth century saw a new wave of nature writing, and it is this movement in which *Pilgrim at Tinker Creek* is frequently placed. Some critics have taken issue with Dillard's identification as a nature writer because of what Linda Smith, author of *Annie Dillard* in Twayne's United States Authors Series, calls her "consistent—even stubborn—devotion to traditional Christianity" and her "concern with aesthetics." But many critics have gone so far as to rank *Pilgrim at Tinker Creek*, as John Tallmadge did in his essay "Beyond the Excursion: Initiatory Themes in Annie Dillard and Terry Tempest Williams," as one of "the most powerful works to appear in the current renaissance of American nature writing."

Critical Overview

Pilgrim at Tinker Creek is widely recognized as an important personal essay, uniquely and powerfully combining theology and nature writing. Nancy Parrish reports in *Lee Smith, Annie Dillard, and the Hollins Group: A Genesis of Writers* that the book's success was immediate: "thirty-seven thousand copies of *Pilgrim* were sold within two months of first publication; the book went through eight printings in the first two years; paperback rights and book-of the-Month Club selection brought her $250,000 within three months." The book was awarded the Pulitzer Prize for general nonfiction.

Most early reviewers responded favorably to the book, including Eva Hoffman, writing for *Commentary,* who termed Dillard a "connoisseur of the spirit" and praised her for her "rare ability to create emotional tone." Others, including the fiction and essay writer Eudora Welty (herself a Pulitzer Prize winner), found Dillard's language and structure needlessly opaque. In a review for the *New York Times Book Review,* Welty quoted Dillard's passage about the "great dog Death" at the end of the "Fecundity" chapter and commented, "I honestly do not know what she is talking about at such times. The only thing I could swear to is that the writing here leaves something to be desired."

Aside from reviews, there was no criticism of the book for several years. In 1983, Margaret

Loewen Reimer's *Critique* article, "The Dialectical Vision of Annie Dillard's *Pilgrim at Tinker Creek*, " initiated a small body of criticism dealing with Dillard's religious themes. This body of criticism, which frequently debates whether Dillard is more an existentialist or a transcendentalist, tends to be written in academic language that makes it difficult for beginning students.

More accessible, and more common, are the critics who address Dillard as a nature writer. Vera Norwood's "Heroines of Nature: Four Women Respond to the American Landscape," in *The Ecocriticism Reader,* examines Dillard as playing an important role in the development of female nature writers and finds that she is among those who "freely choose to seek out wild nature and defend it, thus defying the traditions limiting women access to and appreciation of the natural environment, but who also conclude their explorations in a state of ambivalence." Linda Smith, author of the Twayne's United States Authors series volume *Annie Dillard,* argues that, because of its concern with religion, the book is not primarily nature writing. But James McClintock, in "'Pray Without Ceasing': Annie Dillard among the Nature Writers," disagrees, stating, "Nature writing in America has always been religious or quasi-religious." He concludes that Dillard does belong "among the nature writers" because, "In Dillard's essays, the same persona speaks to us as from the works of other nature writers—the solitary figure in nature, moved to philosophical speculation and, finally, to awe and wonder."

While most critics have admired Dillard's acute powers of observation and her powerful connection with the natural world, more than a few have found her seeming lack of connection with human society unsettling. The poet Hayden Carruth, in his early review in *Virginia Quarterly Review,* found that the book made "little reference to life on this planet at this moment, its hazards and misdirections, and to this extent it is a dangerous book, literally a subversive book." Gary McIlroy acknowledges in his essay " *Pilgrim at Tinker Creek* and the Social Legacy of *Walden*" that this book has less human interaction than the work Dillard patterned it after, *Walden,* but argues that solitude is appropriate for her spiritual quest: "Annie Dillard goes into the woods to claim her spiritual heritage. Like a prophet, she travels alone." In the field of literary criticism about nature writing, Dillard is a major figure. Nearly every significant collection of essays about nature writing, or ecocriticism (the belief that women share a special bond with nature and that both women and nature have been exploited by men) or ecofeminism (the study of literature and the environment) includes an essay about *Pilgrim at Tinker Creek.*

What Do I Read Next?

- Henry David Thoreau's *Walden; or, Life in the Woods,* published in 1854, was Dillard's most important model for *Pilgrim at Tinker Creek.* In *Walden,* Thoreau describes the two years he spent living alone in a cabin on Walden Pond near Concord, Massachusetts, recording his thoughts and his observations of the natural world through the changing seasons.

- *Teaching a Stone to Talk: Expeditions and Encounters* (1982) is a collection of essays by Dillard. These pieces are similar to *Pilgrim at Tinker Creek* in observing and reflecting on the natural world, but they move beyond Virginia as far away as Ecuador.

- *The Writing Life*, published in 1989, is Dillard's exploration of her own creative process and search for an understanding of inspiration. She incorporates literal and metaphorical narratives, including the story of how she composed *Pilgrim at Tinker Creek*.

- Terry Tempest Williams' *An Unspoken Hunger: Stories from the Field* (1995) is a collection of essays about connections between the natural world and our spiritual selves. Most of Williams's essay are set in the American West, and unlike Dillard, she is ever mindful of her place in a human community.

- Another classic work of American nature writing is Henry Beston's 1928 book *The Outermost House: A Year of Life on the Great Beach of Cape Cod.* The book is an account of one year—from autumn to autumn—that Beston spent living alone in a one-room house on the shore of the Atlantic Ocean.

Sources

Carruth, Hayden, "Attractions and Dangers of Nostalgia," in *Virginia Quarterly Review,* Vol. 50, Autumn 1974, p. 640.

Hoffman, Eva, "Solitude," in *Commentary,* Vol. 58, October 1974, p. 87.

Lillard, Richard G., "The Nature Book in Action," in *Teaching Environmental Literature: Materials, Methods, Resources,* edited by Frederick O. Waage, Modern Language Association of America, 1985, p. 36.

McClintock, James I., "'Pray Without Ceasing': Annie Dillard among the Nature Writers," in *Earthly Words: Essays on Contemporary American Nature and Environmental Writers,* edited by John Cooley, University of Michigan Press, 1994, pp. 69, 85.

McIlroy, Gary, " *Pilgrim at Tinker Creek* and the Social Legacy of *Walden,*" in *Earthly Words: Essays on Contemporary American Nature and Environmental Writers,* edited by John Cooley, University of Michigan Press, 1994, p. 100.

Norwood, Vera L., "Heroines of Nature: Four Women Respond to the American Landscape," in *The Ecocriticism Reader: Landmarks in Literary Ecology,* edited by Cheryll Glotfelty and Harold Fromm, University of Georgia Press, 1996, pp. 325-26.

Parrish, Nancy C., *Lee Smith, Annie Dillard, and the Hollins Group: A Genesis of Writers,* Louisiana State University Press, 1998, p. 124.

Reimer, Margaret Loewen, "The Dialectical Vision of Annie Dillard's *Pilgrim at Tinker Creek,*" in *Critique,* Vol. 24, No. 3, Spring 1983, pp. 182-91.

Smith, Linda L., *Annie Dillard,* Twayne, 1991, p. 42.

Tallmadge, John, "Beyond the Excursion: Initiatory Themes in Annie Dillard and Terry Tempest Williams," in *Reading the Earth: New Directions in the Study of Literature and Environment,* edited by Michael P. Branch, Rochelle Johnson, Daniel Patterson, and Scott Slovic, University of Idaho Press, 1998, p. 197.

Thoreau, Henry David, *Walden; or, Life in the Woods,* Dover Thrift, 1995, pp. 65-67, 72.

Welty, Eudora, Review in *New York Times Book Review,* March 24, 1974, p. 4.

Further Reading

McClintock, James I., "'Pray Without Ceasing': Annie Dillard among the Nature Writers," in *Earthly Words: Essays on Contemporary American Nature and Environmental Writers,* edited by John Cooley, University of Michigan Press, 1994, pp. 69-86.

> In this brief essay, McClintock locates two of Dillard's books, *Pilgrim at Tinker Creek* and *Holy the Firm*, within the tradition of American nature writing, focusing on the religious elements of her writing.

Norwood, Vera L., "Heroines of Nature: Four Women Respond to the American Landscape," in *Environmental Review: An International Journal of History and the Humanities,* Vol. 8, Spring 1984, pp. 23-31.

> Norwood traces the differences between men's and women's nature writing in the United States, claiming that while men seek to dominate and conquer the landscape, women tend to embrace and defend it. This article examines writings by Dillard, Rachel Carson, Isabella Bird, and Mary Austin.

Parrish, Nancy L., *Lee Smith, Annie Dillard, and the Hollins Group: A Genesis of Writers,* Louisiana State University Press, 1998.

> Parrish explores the work and lives of a remarkable group of women writers who attended Hollins College in Virginia in the early 1970s. In a chapter entitled "Annie Dillard: *Pilgrim at Tinker Creek,*" she tells some of the stories behind the writing and reveals more intimate personal information than Dillard gives in her own autobiographical works.

Radford, Dawn Evans, "Annie Dillard: A Bibliographical Survey," in *Bulletin of Bibliography,* Vol. 51, No. 2, June 1994, pp. 181-94.

> Radford provides an overview of Dillard's career and of the central issues addressed by critics of her work, followed by an annotated bibliography of nearly two hundred of the most important primary and secondary works. Radford's annotations are succinct and substantive, making this bibliography invaluable for research.

Smith, Linda L., *Annie Dillard,* Twayne's United States Authors Series, 1987.

> Smith's overview is an excellent

starting place for students who wish to learn more about Dillard's life and work. In jargon-free and engaging prose, it presents a brief biography, a chapter about each of Dillard's major books, a chronology of important dates, and an annotated bibliography.

Tietjen, Elaine, "Perceptions of Nature: Annie Dillard's *Pilgrim at Tinker Creek*" in the *North Dakota Quarterly,* Vol. 56, No. 3, Summer 1988, pp. 101-13.

Tietjen gives a personal response to her reading of *Pilgrim at Tinker Creek*, comparing Dillard's reactions to the natural world with her own. Tietjen also had the opportunity to take a class taught by Dillard. She attempts in this essay to make sense of the differences between her idealized conception of Dillard and the real woman and to move beyond her first awestruck reading of the work.

CPSIA information can be obtained
at www.ICGtesting.com
Printed in the USA
LVHW080833090922
727942LV00009B/597